THE OFFICIAL

Study Guide

— & —

Workbook

for

GET OVER
YOUR DAMN SELF

THE NO-BS BLUEPRINT TO BUILDING
A LIFE-CHANGING BUSINESS

ROMI NEUSTADT

Published by:
LiveFullOut Media
www.RomiNeustadt.com

A portion of the profits of every book supports charities that empower the health and education of women and children.

ISBN: 978-0-578-82883-1

CONTENTS

Thank you for daring to design the life you really want. Your guts and grit will not only allow you to step into your greatness, but will also inspire others to do it too. And thank you for believing you're worth it, because you are.

Those are the words of gratitude I wrote in my first book's dedication to you, the Reader. Four years later, I still mean every word, even more deeply.

I wrote *Get Over Your Damn Self* because I wanted to help you build a lucrative and fulfilling direct sales/network marketing business and create a life with more freedom and flexibility, greater purpose and a lot more fun. I've heard from thousands and thousands of you how my book has helped you make the most of this business channel, and expanded how you think about yourself, your life and your possibilities. And it's not just your personal successes you've told me about. You've shared how using *Get Over Your Damn Self* as a team training tool has made onboarding new business partners easier and more efficient and helped your organizations reach new heights.

Requests for a study guide have poured in to help you work through my lessons in the book, both for yourself and your teams. With the demands of my business, my family, writing my second book and the other hats I wear, this project kept getting pushed to the bottom of my to-do list. But with the slower life the pandemic forced, I took everything I learned from you and your book clubs and the *Get Over Your Damn Self* Training Series that I've done for my own team, to create this resource for you. I'm thrilled to give you this Study Guide and Workbook so you have a place to work through and put into action all I teach you in my book.

If you've purchased this without the book because you think you can short cut your way to learning all I have to teach you, I'm not sure you're ready for an entrepreneurial venture. There are no short cuts. But what I can provide you is a blueprint how to work smarter, think bigger and build your business and your life with more confidence. I promise this book will make you laugh (who doesn't need more of that?). And your purchase supports charities that empower the health and education of women and children. #winwin

So grab your copy of *Get Over Your Damn Self* and your team members (and if you don't have any, go find them!) and focus on building your life-changing business. Keep sending me pictures and tagging me on social so I can see your progress, your book clubs and training series. I can't wait to cheer you on. And just like my book, I hope you return to this tool again and again to restart, refresh and recommit to your business and to keep getting over your damn self. Because we humans need that.

Let's go!

XO,

Romi

**Make a commitment
to be 100% coachable.**

CHAPTER 1

Why People Fail and Why That Ain't Gonna Be You

The 4 reasons people fail:

1. _____

2. _____

3. _____

4. _____

Which of these could trip you up?

_____

How many hours per week will you be dedicating to your business? _____

Where to spend your time building your business:

80% = _____

10% = _____

10% = _____

Get in Action

☐ Declare it loudly right now: "I am 100% coachable!"

You need a bulletproof
WHY to get you through
the tough times. And
that WHY has to be
about you and for you.

CHAPTER 2
Why Are You Here?

What is your WHY?

_____

_____

_____

_____

_____

Why is this so important to you? Get really specific here. How do you see this changing your life, affecting your family, helping you get where you want to be long-term?

_____

_____

_____

_____

_____

Our WHYs evolve along with our businesses, and the key to consistent growth and not stalling out is to continually check in with yourself and your priorities.

If you don't achieve your WHY, what's your pain you'll experience? In other words, what's the cost you'll pay in your life by NOT taking action to build this business? Really flesh out this part. What will you and your family miss out on in life? How will this affect your confidence and your self esteem?

_____

_____

_____

_____

_____

Look ahead five years into the future. If you don't achieve your WHY, where will you be, and what will you have given up, all because you didn't follow through and take action on what was important?

_____

_____

_____

_____

Get in Action

☐ Read what you wrote above every day for 3 weeks.

The best thing you can do for
yourself and your future
business partners is to keep
a very thorough Master List.

CHAPTER 3

Your List Is Your Life: Make It a Long One

Your Dirt List:

1. _____

2. _____

3. _____

4. _____

5. _____

Your Master List

You can start your list in this workbook (starting on page 17), a notebook or a contact management app like Penny.

Make a list of everyone you know from:

* Community leaders, movers and shakers
* People you went to school with (elementary, middle, high, college)
* Church, synagogue or temple
* Friends of friends
* My spouse's or boyfriend's network
* Past and present work colleagues
* Dinner parties, bridal showers, weddings, graduations
* People who provide you services: accountants, Fed-Ex Delivery, nail tech, plumber
* Professionals: educators, health care professionals, lawyers, real estate agents
* Non-profit boards and volunteers
* Social media contacts: Facebook, LinkedIn, Instagram
* Chamber of Commerce members/ events

You'll likely think of new people every day, and at least once a month you should sit down and methodically add people to your list.

* Moms' groups, stay-at-home moms
* Groups: book clubs, bunco groups, happy hour groups
* People with hobbies: golfers, tennis players, gardeners, equestrians, cyclists, hikers
* Political activist groups
* Parents of kids' classmates
* Parents in all kids' activities (sports, clubs, religious school)
* Teachers, coaches, instructors, mentors
* People on trains, planes, and automobiles
* Active military or military spouses
* Swimming pool loungers and coffee shop regulars
* Neighbors and former neighbors
* People who sell stuff: real estate, cars, retail
* People who love the arts: symphony, opera, fine art, ballet patrons
* People whose business you support or have supported
* People who get things done
* My brother's network, my sister's network
* My parents' networks

Think about you who know with the following names:

Ann, Allison, Abby
Bonnie, Brenda, Barbara
Christine, Catherine, Cara
Diane, Debbie, Dana
Elizabeth, Elise, Eliana
Faith, Finlay, Felicia
Gina, Gabrielle, Grace
Helen, Hannah, Heather
Isabel, Ivy, Iliana

Jill, Jacqueline, Julia
Kathy, Kim, Kate
Laurie, Lisa, Leah
Melanie, Megan, Maria
Nancy, Nikki, Natalie
Olivia, Opal, Octavia
Patricia, Penny, Paula
Quinn, Quincy, Queen
Rachel, Rebecca, Rosie

Stephanie, Samantha, Sofia
Tina, Tiffany, Tonya
Uma, Unity, Una
Valerie, Vanessa, Vida
Wendy, Willow, Whitney
Xena, Xanthi, Xyla
Yvonne, Yvette, Yasmine
Zena, Zoe, Zara

Do the alphabet again with male names.

Add your Chicken List (the people you're scared to talk to). Remember, don't be a chicken shit!

The best thing you can do for
yourself and your future
business partners is to keep
a very thorough Master List.

MASTER LIST

1. _____

2. _____

3. _____

4. _____

5. _____

6. _____

7. _____

8. _____

9. _____

10. _____

11. _____

12. _____

13. _____

14. _____

15. _____

16. _____

17. _____

18. _____

19. _____

20. _____

21. _____

22. _____

23. _____

24. _____

25. _____

26. _____

27. _____

28. _____

29. _____

30. _____

31. _____

32. _____

33. _____

34. _____

35. _____

36. _____

37. _____

38. _____

39. _____

40. _____

Listen for opportunities
to offer up solutions to
someone's problem.

41. _____

42. _____

43. _____

44. _____

45. _____

46. _____

47. _____

48. _____

49. _____

50. _____

51. _____

52. _____

53. _____

54. _____

55. _____

56. _____

57. _____

58. _____

59. _____

60. _____

61. _____

62. _____

63. _____

64. _____

65. _____

66. _____

67. _____

68. _____

69. _____

70. _____

71. _____

72. _____

73. _____

74. _____

75. _____

76. _____

77. _____

78. _____

79. _____

80. _____

81. _____

82. _____

83. _____

84. _____

None of us know what anyone is thinking, so all the time and energy you spend speculating is a waste.

85. _____

86. _____

87. _____

88. _____

89. _____

90. _____

91. _____

92. _____

93. _____

94. _____

95. _____

96. _____

97. _____

98. _____

99. _____

100. _____

101. _____

102. _____

103. _____

104. _____

105. _____

106. _____

107. _____

108. _____

109. _____

110. _____

111. _____

112. _____

113. _____

114. _____

115. _____

116. _____

117. _____

118. _____

119. _____

120. _____

121. _____

122. _____

123. _____

124. _____

125. _____

126. _____

127. _____

128. _____

We're paid storytellers.
So the better you are at
telling your story, the
more successful you'll be.

CHAPTER 4
What's Your Story

CRAFT YOUR STORY

1. Who you are and where you've been.

_____

_____

_____

_____

2. What's happened in your life to cause you to look for something more.

_____

_____

_____

_____

3. How you heard about your company and why you had to be a part of it.

_____

_____

_____

_____

People are drawn to authenticity, so don't be afraid to share your real story, even before it's totally comfortable to do so.

4. What's it doing for you or going to do for you. (Include quantifiables.)

_____

_____

_____

_____

MY STORY

Put it all together. And revisit your story to tweak it _at least_ once a quarter.

_____

_____

_____

_____

_____

_____

_____

_____

_____

_____

_____

Figure out a person's
pain points and how our
business can reduce or
eliminate her pain.

CHAPTER 5

How I Talked My Way to Seven Figures and How You Can Too

Which of the Reach-Out Rules have you been violating?

_____

_____

_____

_____

Get in Action

What's In It For Them (WIIFT)

Name:_____

PAIN	NO PAIN

Name:_____

PAIN	NO PAIN

Name:_____

PAIN	NO PAIN

Name:_____

PAIN	NO PAIN

Name:_____

PAIN	NO PAIN

Name:_____

PAIN	NO PAIN

Name:_____

PAIN	NO PAIN

Name:_____

PAIN	NO PAIN

Name:_____

PAIN	NO PAIN

Name:_____

PAIN	NO PAIN

Everything you say and do should be motivated by helping someone come to the right decision for them.

She's Interested...Now What?

CONVERSATION FLOWCHART

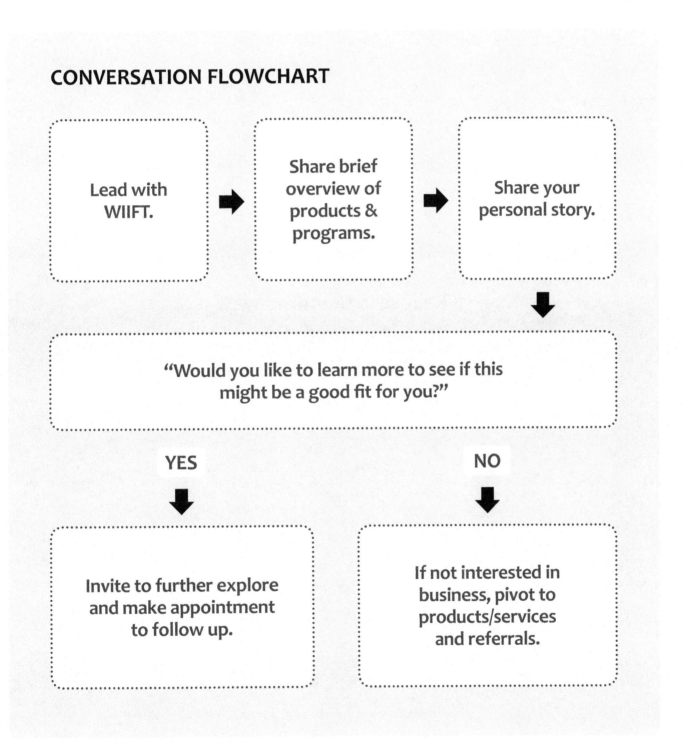

Believe in the three-way.
Crave the three-way.
Master the three-way.

What can you invite your prospect to in order to learn more (event, videos, three-way call)?

_____

_____

_____

_____

Always set the next _____ before leaving the current conversation.

Get in Action

Set up 3 three-way calls with your upline in the next week.

☐ CALL 1: Name _____ Date_____ Time_____

☐ CALL 2: Name _____ Date_____ Time_____

☐ CALL 3: Name _____ Date_____ Time_____

People often don't really understand what they're objecting to or they have incorrect assumptions.

CHAPTER 7

I OBJECT!

The 2 most important things to remember when handling objections are:

1. _____

2. _____

For each objection, write the corresponding clarifying question that will help you get more information about what your prospect is really thinking.

I don't think I have enough time to do this.

Clarifying question: _____

I don't have the money to do this.

Clarifying question: _____

I don't want to bother friends.

Clarifying question: _____

I don't know enough people.

Clarifying question: _____

I'm not a salesperson.

Clarifying question: _____

The timing just isn't right for me to start a business.

Clarifying question: _____

Is this a pyramid?

Clarifying question: _____

I've found the best way
to get someone to decide
is to spoonfeed them a
decision-making process.

CHAPTER 8

She's Just Not That
Into You...Or Is She?

Write out the questions to use to bring a prospect to a decision.

1. _____

2. _____

3. _____

Write out a Take Away you can use when necessary.

_____

_____

_____

_____

What homework will you assign to someone who's undecided?

_____

_____

_____

_____

**People need to see or
hear your message
many, many times
before they take action.**

CHAPTER 9

The Fortune's in the Follow-Up

Fill in the Blanks:

No actually means "_____ _____ _____."

Failure comes not from getting No, but from failing to _____ with the No.

The Golden Rule: Reach back out periodically to _____ unless they've

already _____ or told you "_____."

Who are your lowest hanging fruit for finding business builders/referrals?

_____

People you talk to are programmed by human nature and their environment to say No the

first time, so their No says _____ about you!

Which system will you use to keep track of your Master List and follow ups?

☐ Excel/Google Drive spreadsheet   ☐ Word/Google Drive doc

☐ Notebook   ☐ Contact Management App (like Penny)

☐ Index Cards

I like to think of reaching
back to people as a game.
It's fun to figure out
excuses to loop back.

List reasons to reach back to people.

1. _____

2. _____

3. _____

4. _____

5. _____

6. _____

7. _____

8. _____

9. _____

10. _____

Get in Action

Every day for the next six days, pick one of the reasons and think about who you can reach back to using that reason as a hook. Shoot for at least three people for each reason. Incorporate this exercise into your weekly activities, even making one day each week "Reach-Back Day." You'll train yourself to constantly think of reasons, and make it a routine part of your business.

To build big you must commit
today to be the top producer
on your team.

CHAPTER 10

The Key to Duplication

What are the 5 things you need to be doing to start the duplication process?

1. _____

2. _____

3. _____

4. _____

5. _____

Based on The Half Rule, what volume can you expect your team to do?

_____

_____

What is the minimum personal volume goal you commit to, especially in light of The Half Rule? And what biz building habits are you willing to do to get there?

_____

_____

_____

The next time you find
yourself saying "I don't
have time," instead try
saying "It's not a priority,"
and see how that feels.

CHAPTER 11
The Bullshit We Tell Ourselves

What BS are you telling yourself?

1. _____

What's the truth? _____

_____

2. _____

What's the truth? _____

_____

3. _____

What's the truth? _____

_____

4. _____

What's the truth? _____

_____

So why don't you have enough time to reach out and talk to people? Because it's hard. But here's the thing: it's the hard stuff that's the most important.

5. _____

What's the truth? _____

_____

6. _____

What's the truth? _____

_____

7. _____

What's the truth? _____

_____

8. _____

What's the truth? _____

_____

9. _____

What's the truth? _____

_____

This biz is a numbers
game, and there's no way
to bullshit the numbers.

If you or a member of your team isn't growing (or is going backwards), what 2 questions should you ask yourself or her?

1. How many times have you _____ this week?

2. How many _____ have you done this week?

List 5 things you must do to grow a lucrative business.

1. _____

2. _____

3. _____

4. _____

5. _____

Get in Action

☐ Make a list of all the things you spend time doing for your business over the next week.

☐ Take a red pen to all the things that don't fall in the list above.

☐ Schedule in the hard stuff – dedicated time to reach out and talk to people about your business and your products.

When you ignore your
gut, that's when you
get into trouble.

CHAPTER 12

Karma's a Bitch if You Are

What is the Golden Rule to live and build your biz by?

_____

_____

What are you going to say when you talk to someone who already has talked to or is talking to another business builder in your company?

_____

_____

What are things you've done, but now that you know better, you're going to do better?

_____

_____

_____

_____

Say this daily: "I know what my time is worth and someone has to be all in to get my time."

CHAPTER 13

Your Time is Worth $962 an Hour

How much is YOUR time worth?

1. How much do you ultimately want to earn annually from your business?

_____

(Don't limit yourself to what you want to bring in next month or next year. I'm talking the BIG NUMBER. What do you want this business to grow into?)

2. How many hours a week do you want to work?_____

(I'm not talking what you think **have** to work. You need to be honest about how many hours you **want** to work every week on your business.)

3. Use these numbers to come up with your time's hourly worth.

_____ hours per week x 52 weeks = _____ hours per year

(annual income) / _____ hours per year = $ _____ per hour

Every hour of my time is worth $_____!

If you're finding it hard to find time for personal prospecting, then you're doing too much of something else.

What's on your Stop Doing List?

_____

_____

_____

_____

_____

_____

_____

_____

What will you do to diminish your distractions?

_____

_____

_____

_____

_____

Combining activities can help
us achieve our goals without
maxing ourselves out.

What questions will you cover during all your coaching calls with your team for efficiency and to frame conversations?

_____

_____

_____

_____

_____

_____

What multipliers are you going to implement?

_____

_____

_____

_____

_____

_____

_____

The problem with
Shoulds is they don't
support our priorities.

CHAPTER 14

Taking Care of You Along the Way

What do you want to say No to right now?

_____

_____

_____

_____

What help are you going to get for yourself?

_____

_____

_____

_____

What personal development do you commit to?

_____

_____

_____

_____

In a business where we must
be magnetic and patient and
resilient, downtime is essential.

What exercise do you commit to (what and when)? And then put it on your calendar!

_____

_____

_____

_____

What downtime do you commit to (what and when)? And then put it on your calendar!

_____

_____

_____

_____

When will you turn your phone off every day? _____

How will you celebrate your little victories? Write down the accomplishment and how you'll reward yourself.

_____

_____

_____

_____

If they know not only WHY
you're building your business,
but also what's in it for them,
it will make it easier for them
to accept the new normal of
you and your side biz.

CHAPTER 15
It's a Family Affair

What are the ways that growing your business will help your spouse/partner and/or family?

_____

_____

_____

_____

If you have kids, how can you include them in your business?

_____

_____

_____

_____

Get in Action

☐ Share the list of WIIFT (What's In It For Them) with your family tonight.

☐ Meet with your spouse/partner this week to have them create a list and decide the best way to connect you.

It's not our job to argue with fear or fix it or escape it. It's our job to act in spite of it.

CHAPTER 16
#FUCKFEAR

What are your top 5 fears when it comes to building your business?

1. _____

2. _____

3. _____

4. _____

5. _____

Remind yourself of your WHY. Make sure your WHY is important enough that the fear of NOT achieving it is bigger than any of your other fears.

_____

_____

_____

Get in Action

☐ Write down on a piece of paper all your fears about your business and your ability to build it, and then burn or shred that paper. The fears won't magically disappear, but you'll let go of their hold over you.

WANT MORE ROMI IN YOUR LIFE?

Read her blog at RomiNeustadt.com.

Follow her on Instagram @RomiNeustadt
and Facebook @RomiNeustadtBiz.

Read her second book, *You Can Have It All, Just Not at the Same Damn Time*, her no-BS blueprint to teach you how to figure out what you really want in life, how to focus on that and let go of everything else.

Listen to her read both her books on Audible.

* * * * *

If you enjoyed this workbook/study guide, please spend a few minutes writing a review on Amazon.

Made in the USA
Middletown, DE
19 January 2021

31971518R00040